Living Th
Everywhere!

Jayne Smith

ABRAMS & COMPANY Publishers, Inc.
Waterbury, CT

Contents

Living things are everywhere!

How many can you find?

Living things grow.

Babies grow into adults.

Seeds grow into plants.

Which of these things grow?

Living things need food.

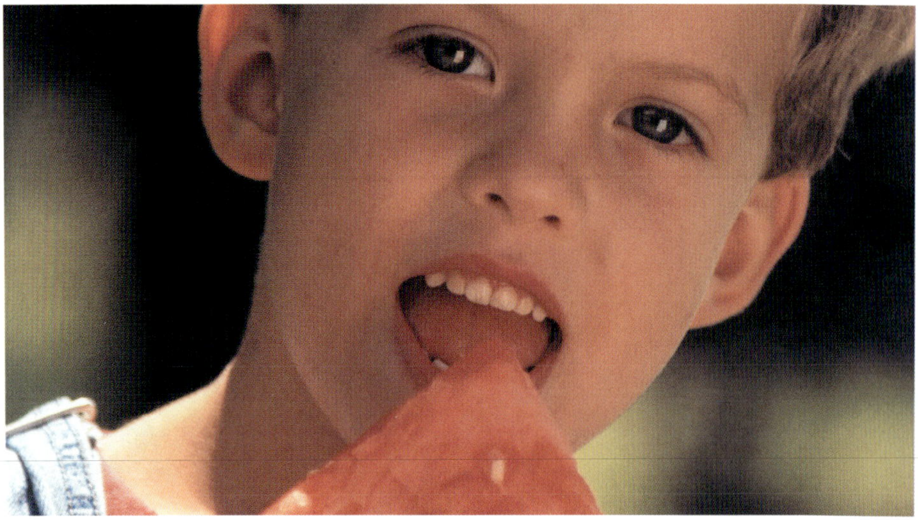

People eat food.

Plants make food in their leaves.

Which of these things need food?

Living things breathe.

People breathe through mouths and noses.

Fish breathe through gills.

Plants breathe through openings in their leaves.

Which of these things breathe?

Living things make more of their own kind.

People and animals have babies.

Plants make seeds that grow into new plants.

Which of these things make more of their own kind?

Living things grow.

Living things need food.

Living things breathe.

Living things make more of their own kind.

Which of these are living things?

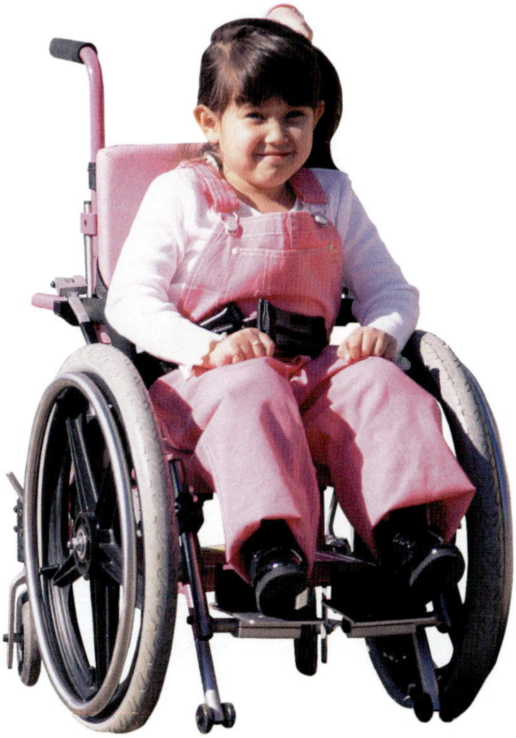

Find some living and nonliving things.